COMMUNITY • CONNECTIONS

HOW DO WE LIVE TOGETHER?
COYOTES

BY KATIE MARSICO

Published in the United States of America by Cherry Lake Publishing
Ann Arbor, Michigan
www.cherrylakepublishing.com

Content Adviser: Stephen S. Ditchkoff, PhD, Associate Professor, School of Forestry and
Wildlife Sciences, Auburn University
Reading Adviser: Cecilia Minden-Cupp, PhD, Literacy Consultant

Photo Credits: Cover and page 1, ©Outdoorsman/Dreamstime.com; page 5, ©Liga Alksne,
used under license from Shutterstock, Inc.; page 7, ©Boris Z., used under license from
Shutterstock, Inc.; page 9, ©iStockphoto.com/RoseMaryBush; page 11, ©Ronnie Howard, used
under license from Shutterstock, Inc.; page 13, ©iStockphoto.com/JudiLen; page 15, ©Nelson
Hale, used under license from Shutterstock, Inc.; page 17, ©Bigsky06/Dreamstime.com;
page 19, ©FredS, used under license from Shutterstock, Inc.; page 21, ©nialat, used under
license from Shutterstock, Inc.

LIBRARY OF CONGRESS CATALOGING-IN-PUBLICATION DATA
Marsico, Katie, 1980–
  How do we live together? Coyotes / by Katie Marsico.
    p. cm.—(Community connections)
  Includes bibliographical references and index.
  ISBN-13: 978-1-60279-621-8
  ISBN-10: 1-60279-621-1
  1. Coyote—Juvenile literature. I. Title. II. Title: Coyotes.
III. Series.
  QL737.C22M3643 2010
  599.77'25—dc22   2009022425

Cherry Lake Publishing would like to acknowledge the
work of The Partnership for 21st Century Skills. Please
visit *www.21stcenturyskills.org* for more information.

Printed in the United States of America
Corporate Graphics Inc.
January 2010
CLSP06

CONTENTS

4 Is That Someone's Dog?

10 A Closer Look at Coyotes

16 Sharing Outdoor Spaces

22 Glossary

23 Find Out More

24 Index

24 About the Author

IS THAT SOMEONE'S DOG?

You let your puppy run in the backyard every morning. Today you peek outside and see something. It looks like another dog moving through the grass. You realize that you are staring at a coyote! You decide to keep your pet inside. He won't be safe outside until this wild animal is gone.

Coyotes look a lot like dogs.

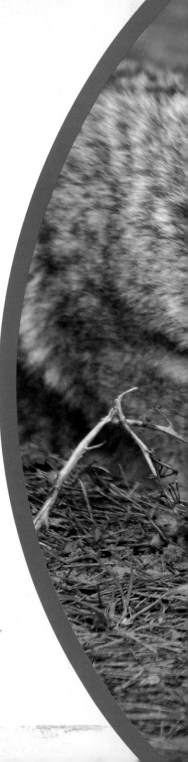

Draw a picture of a dog. Then compare it to a picture of a coyote. How are the pictures alike? How are they different?

Why would it have been unsafe to let your dog outside? Coyotes are **territorial**. This means they claim an area of land as their own. They attack other animals to protect this territory. The coyote may think your yard is part of its territory. Your dog may be in danger if the coyote sees him there.

Coyotes keep watch to be sure other animals aren't in their territory.

Sometimes coyotes attack other animals. Coyotes are **predators**. They might eat a farmer's sheep or chickens. This is why many humans do not like coyotes. They are afraid their animals will be hurt or killed.

How can we safely share the outdoors with coyotes? Learning more about coyotes will help keep animals and people safe.

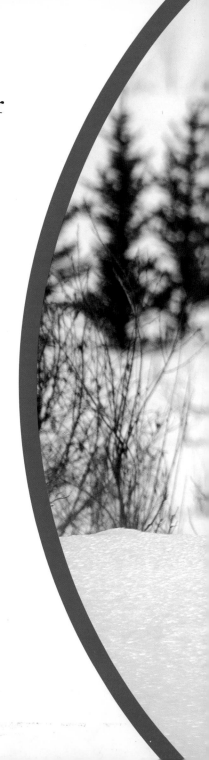

This coyote is trying to catch its dinner!

A CLOSER LOOK AT COYOTES

Have you ever seen a coyote up close? It might have been in a zoo or a wildlife park. Did you notice how much it looked like a fox or a wolf? These animals are all **mammals**. They are closely related to one another.

The sound of a coyote howling can be loud.

Have you ever heard an animal howling at night? Can you guess what kind of animal was making this noise? It might have been a coyote! Howling is one way they talk to each other.

Coyotes are found in North America and Central America. Their **prey** includes rabbits and squirrels. They also eat birds and deer. Sometimes they eat berries and fruits. They also like plants and seeds. Coyotes find their food in the wild. So why do they come around humans?

Coyotes can run as fast as 40 miles (64 kilometers) per hour.

Coyotes do not have enough space. There are too many of them. They have trouble finding enough food. Many coyotes look for new territories. Some end up near humans.

Most people do not want animal predators living near them. Living near people is not always safe for coyotes. Is there a solution to this problem?

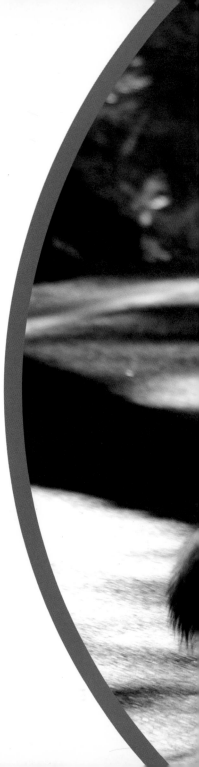

Crossing streets can be dangerous for coyotes.

SHARING OUTDOOR SPACES

Some people believe killing coyotes is the answer. Not everyone agrees, though. Others think they are helpful animals. They want to protect coyotes. They work to help preserve **wilderness** areas for animals. If wilderness areas are larger, coyotes will have more space. Then fewer coyotes will need to seek food in towns.

Wilderness areas are the best places for coyotes to live.

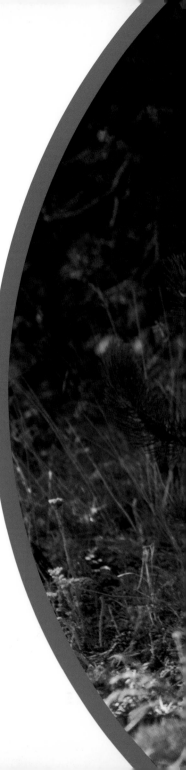

Can you think of ways that coyotes help humans? One way is by hunting prey such as mice and rats. These animals can often spread **diseases**. Coyotes help keep the number of mice and rats from growing too large.

How can you help? Keep your garbage cans tightly sealed. Keep pet food inside the house. Garbage and pet food make easy meals for a coyote. Walk your pet on a leash outside. Keep your pet indoors at night. Coyotes are most active when it is dark.

Don't be tempted to feed coyotes! They may look like dogs, but they are wild animals.

Do not feed the coyotes.

Remember that you can make a difference. There are many simple ways you can help humans and coyotes share the outdoors. Can you think of a few more?

Coyotes are wonderful animals. We can learn to safely live together.

Local wildlife experts may have other tips about how to live with coyotes. Next time you visit a nature center or zoo, ask the experts some questions. Asking questions is a good way to learn more.

GLOSSARY

diseases (duh-ZEEZ-ehz) kinds of illnesses

mammals (MAM-uhlz) warm-blooded animals that are usually covered in hair, have a backbone, give birth to live young, and make milk to feed their babies

predators (PRED-uh-turz) animals that hunt and kill other animals for food

prey (PRAY) animals that are hunted and eaten by predators

territorial (ter-uh-TOHR-ee-uhl) claiming an area of land and protecting it from other animals

wilderness (WILL-dur-niss) an area of land that stays mostly untouched by humans

FIND OUT MORE

BOOKS

Hodge, Deborah. *Wild Dogs: Wolves, Coyotes, and Foxes.*
Toronto: Kids Can Press, 2009.

Macken, JoAnn Early. *Coyotes.* Pleasantville, NY: Weekly Reader,
2010.

WEB SITES

National Geographic Kids—Animals Creature Feature: Coyotes
kids.nationalgeographic.com/Animals/CreatureFeature/Coyote
Read more about how coyotes live and hunt.

Wolf Park: Kids—Coyote Stuff
www.wolfparkkids.org/animals/coyotestuff.html
Learn about how coyotes are related to wolves.

INDEX

chickens, 8

darkness, 18
diseases, 17
dogs, 4, 5, 6

foods, 12, 14, 16,
   17, 18
foxes, 10

garbage, 18

howling, 11

mammals, 10
mice, 17

people, 8, 14, 16,
   17, 20
pets, 4, 6, 18

predators, 8, 14
prey, 12, 17

rats, 17

sheep, 8

territories, 6, 14
towns, 16

wilderness areas,
   16
wildlife experts, 21
wolves, 10

ABOUT THE AUTHOR

Katie Marsico is the author of more than 50 children's books and lives in Elmhurst, Illinois, with her husband and three children. She occasionally spots a coyote in her own neighborhood.